D1798639

The Weird and Wonderful World of...

ANIMALS

Managing Editors: Simon Melhuish

Series Editor: Nikole G Bamford

Design and Cover: Linley J Clode

Cartoons: Randy Glasbergen

Published by
The Lagoon Group
PO Box 311, KT2 5QW, UK
PO Box 990676, Boston, MA 02199, USA

ISBN: 1905439660

© 2006 LAGOON BOOKS

www.thelagoongroup.com

Printed in China

The Weird and Wonderful World of...

ANIMALS

"My therapy is quite simple: I wag my tail and lick your face until you feel good about yourself again."

"I taught him how to shake hands. The business cards were his own idea."

"I never wanted to be a seagull. I wanted to be an eagle, but my guidance counselor was really lame."

"He pretended to throw the ball, but he faked me out. It was the most humiliating experience of my life. But now I'm learning to live with the pain, one day at a time."

"I tried all the fitness fads, but my doctor was
right all along—walking is still the best exercise."

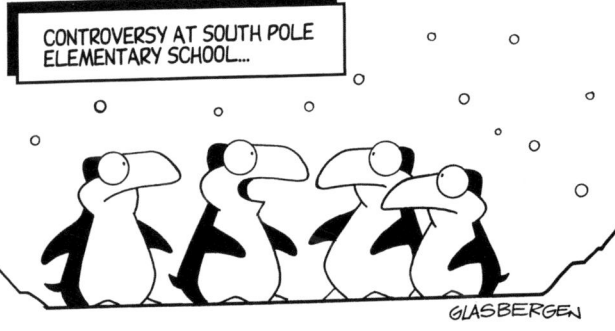

"Did you hear? They might make us
wear uniforms to school next year!"

"I jumped over the moon, for pete sake!
I should be swamped with endorsement offers,
but all I got was a stupid nursery rhyme!
You're a lousy agent, Bernie!"

"Looks aren't everything. It's what's inside you that really matters. A biology teacher told me that."

"If swimming is good for developing shoulders, arms and legs, why haven't we developed any shoulders, arms and legs?"

"*Cats*—the fragrance for dogs who dare to be different!"

"You could have brought home a canary or a goldfish, but you chose me instead. So you see, the stain on the carpet is actually *your* fault."

"This exercise is great for your arms, shoulders, chest and back. Do four sets of 15 repetitions, then move on to the yarn ball for your aerobics."

GLASBERGEN

"No dolphin ever spent $2,000 just to play silly games on a computer that will be obsolete in six months. That *proves* we're smarter than humans!"

Einstein's cat.

"When do they take us out to go to the bathroom?
I don't think I can hold it much longer!"

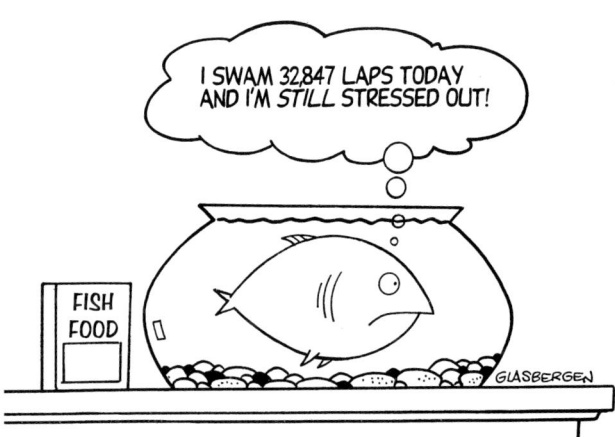

"The colored stones were fine when we were
first married, but isn't it about time
we got some real furniture?"

"It's an organ donor card. If you go first, I'd like to get your bones."

"I never imagined he'd get this big. When we
brought him home, we thought he was a guinea pig."

"When you're done ruining the sofa, I want you to start clawing the new stereo speakers. After that, you need to leave your tongue prints in the butter, then take a nap on a pile of clean laundry."

"Licking your paws is just the first step.
After that, you need to use a good antibacterial
body wash, then an exfoliating herbal facial scrub,
followed by avocado moisturizing cleanser...."

"Grandpa, tell me again about
the time you caught an airplane!"

"I know you hid my pill in the cheese.
How stupid do you think I am?"

"Hold the sock tight in your mouth, then race from room to room as fast as you can—it's the greatest stress management technique ever!"

"Section six twisted his ankle and has
to stay off his feet for a month."

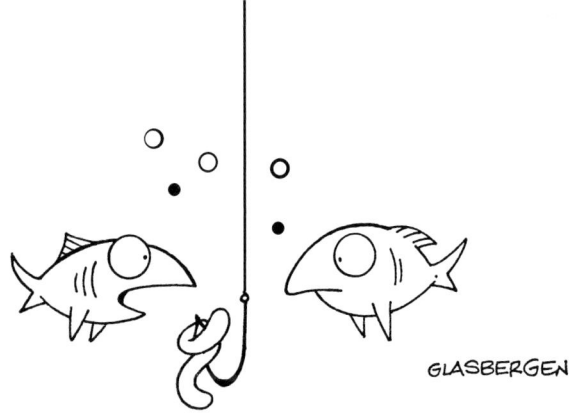

"You eat the worm, then you floss with the string!"

GLASBERGEN

"MY COUSIN SHIRLEY VOLUNTEERED FOR DISSECTION.
SHE THOUGHT SHE COULD CONVINCE THEM TO DO
A FACELIFT AND A TUMMY TUCK INSTEAD."

"Actually, I'm 60% leaner than you.
I'm made from turkey!"

"They say we're not placing enough emphasis on diversity."

"Having nine lives is cool, but if I have to
go through menopause again, forget it!"

"If you kids would do more to help out around the house, I'd have time to fix something besides *worms* for dinner!"

"I belong to a cult that believes cats have nine lives."

"The funny walk and tuxedo feathers are my intellectual
property and trademark. If you want to look or act
like me, you have to pay me a million dollars."

"While we're on the subject of retirement planning, have you set aside enough money to have me cloned?"

"I'm enjoying a very happy retirement and
I never invested a cent! Ha ha ha ha ha ha ha!"

"SON, I KNOW TEENAGERS LIKE TO BE DIFFERENT, BUT WHEN YOU DRESS LIKE THAT, YOUR MOTHER AND I GET SO EMBARRASSED!"

"I have 30,000 fish saved for my retirement. I'd like to roll them over into something that doesn't stink to high heaven!"

"I can get by on just 2 hours of sleep
every day, as long as I nap for 14 hours."

"Today I ate two bowls of dog food, a sandwich crust, some spaghetti that fell on the floor, half of your catfood, a wet tea bag, three bugs and the inside of a shoe. How many grams of fat is that?"

"I found an Arts and Crafts site that shows how to turn hairballs into cherished gifts for the whole family!"

"After the hunt, could you stop off and get me some zebra nuggets and a gazelle shake?"

"We'd like tonight to be special.
Could you get some water from the toilet
and put it in a champagne bottle?"

"Don't worry...I'm just practicing my yoga!"

"Remember the Golden Rule: Drool unto others
as you would have them drool unto you!"

"Howl at an ambulance or fire siren every chance you get. Run around the room in circles with a sock in your mouth. Eat a messy meal without using your hands or utensils. Ask a friend to scratch your belly..."

"Low fat diets don't work. I eat fish every day
and my butt still drags on the ground!"

CLICK

"I need some medical advice.
Go to www.cheese-with-a-pill-in-it.com!"

"The government says your breath is destroying the ozone."

"My personal trainer said Yoga would give me longer, sexier muscles, but it didn't work for me."

"It's true, I did jump over the moon.
I had waaaaay too much coffee that day!"

"A Canine-American who's paid six figures. Imagine
how good that would look in your diversity profile!"

"Can't we just talk without you dissecting every word I say?"

"Try www.pet-stains.com!"

"In dog years, one hour equals six months
when you're waiting to be fed!"

"I'm sorry, son, but I don't like those friends you hang out with. They look like the type of hoodlums who would shed on the good sofa, chew socks, and drink from the toilet!"

"Eat, sleep, eat, sleep...I don't know how
much longer I can keep up this insane pace!"

"I think he's spending too much time with the kids."

"Experts say that petting a cat is a good way to reduce stress...but nobody told the cat!"

"I've outsourced my job to a dog overseas
who will be your companion via web cam."

"With all the cool electronic toys and video games
in this house, why are we playing with a ball of yarn?"

"Your owners pet you to relieve stress. If that fails, you could
be sued for malpractice. That's why you need cat insurance."

"Did you ever notice that there's a million cats named 'Mittens' but none named 'Scarf', 'Hat', or 'Snowsuit'?"

"I'm here to talk to you about outsourcing. I have 15,000 friends who are willing to work for fish and blankets!"

"I listened to some motivational tapes while you
were at work and I've decided to become a Great Dane!"

"If you sign up at $29.95 a month, you get 20 minutes of outdoor play, 15 face licks, and unlimited tail wagging on nights and weekends. For $49.95 a month, you get..."

"You're allowed up to 5 cell phones on your family calling plan. Where's mine?"

"I can't wear a watch on my tiny wrist, so I never know
when it's time to get up. That's why I sleep all day."

"Eat, sleep, eat, sleep, eat, sleep. Do you really
need to write all of this down in your Daily Planner?"

"In one way or another, we're all confined by invisible fencing."

"You and I are both Aquarius. Our horoscope says it's a good day to ask for a raise and lick our feet."

"Your mother and I have a happy marriage because we love each other...
plus it's too hard to drive downtown to see a lawyer."

"Of course cats can talk! We just don't talk to humans
because we don't care about politics, sports, TV,
or what color dress J.Lo wore last night."

"Jumping from the sofa to the bookcase to the top
of the grandfather clock was a lot more fun
before they made me wear a helmet!"

DOG COMEDY

"FLEAS! Fleas are the worst! They live all over me...
but do I ever get a rent check?! And their parties
keep me up ALL NIGHT! Fleas have terrible taste
in music! On their tiny speakers everything sounds
like Alvin and the Chipmunks singing Michael Jackson!"

"I don't scratch my fleas. I'm afraid of their lawyers!"

"Got any books about time management?
I'd like to schedule more naps into my day."

"I told you people love penguins! We haven't
been sued once since we made him our CEO."